FINDING JOY IN Loneliness

BRITTANI KREBBS

ADOWN PUBLISHING
SEATTLE WASHINGTON

FINDING JOY IN LONELINESS

Copyright © 2020 by Brittani Krebbs

Scripture quotations marked NIV are taken from The Holy Bible, *New International Version*, *NIV*. Copyright © 1973, 1978, 1984, 2011 by Biblica, Inc.™ Used by permission. All rights reserved worldwide.

Scripture quotations marked NLT are taken from the *Holy Bible, New Living Translation*, copyright © 1996, 2004. Used by permission of Tyndale House Publishers, Inc., Wheaton, Illinois. All rights reserved.

Scripture quotations marked ESV are taken from The ESV® Bible (The Holy Bible, English Standard Version®), copyright © 2001 by Crossway, a publishing ministry of Good News Publishers. Used by permission. All rights reserved.

Scripture taken from the New King James Version®. Copyright © 1982 by Thomas Nelson. Used by permission. All rights reserved.

Cover Photography by Amanda Long

Cover Design by Michaela McIntosh

Wheat Illustration by Peter Leach

ISBN: 978-1-7358261-0-3 Paperback

ISBN: 978-1-7358261-1-0 eBook

www.brittanikrebbs.com

Printed in the United States of America

TABLE OF CONTENTS

PROLOGUE

"I don't feel lonely, because I have the Lord."

WHAT A LIE! (Well, maybe not a lie, but definitely not the whole truth)...

Has anyone else thought this? I sure have! Once I became a believer, I thought all my deep-hearted problems and trauma would go away just like that! Welp, I was wrong... As you will read in this book, I believed life as a Christian was supposed to be one big fairy tale. I will tell you 100% that Jesus IS the answer, and we CAN find joy in our loneliness. However, ignoring the hurt and stuffing down the past so that you can put on a "happy facade," is not who we are called to be in Christ Jesus.

The quote above came from my very first YouTube video in 2015. I was a college student majoring in Converged Broadcast Media at UNT, and I wanted to bring hope, joy and Jesus to the military community. I searched and searched, but couldn't find any encouraging videos like the ones I wanted to share, so I went ahead and posted my first one. Within the first day, it got hundreds of views! And let me tell you, each time I checked, and the number got higher, I would do a little happy dance. Even 200 views was exciting, and now it sits at almost 300,000 views! Honestly, I had no idea that would happen, but I knew I needed to continue.

A few months after that very first video I began to receive emails from people expressing their appreciation or asking me for advice.

"I just stumbled upon your YouTube channel and I just wanted to say THANK YOU for your channel! You Are so positive and inspiring and watching your videos has uplifted me."

She later mentions in her email:

"If you have any kind of advice I would so appreciate it!

Thank you for taking the time to read this!"

I'm crying right now and by faith, (not a coincidence) I came across your videos. I'm still sad because I miss him and hearing his voice so much. I'm worried but your videos spoke to me and filled some of the hole I have in my heart. I feel like God guided me to watch your videos because He knows how much I need to vent to someone who will understand me and help me through this. Please pray for God to give me strength and for God to bless my relationship because we really want this to work out. I really hope to hear from you. God bless you for your videos and your very kind heart! I will be praying for you and your husband Con because NOW I understand how hard, but how worth it, it is."

"So, I was hoping reaching out to you would make me feel less alone and help me find some encouragement to keep pushing on when it gets hard."

Emails like this continued to come in with women asking for advice and sharing their stories. I always questioned why they would email me. A random girl on the internet sitting on the floor of her college duplex. I realized later it was because I gave them hope, but more importantly, they felt less lonely. They desired to connect with someone. They wanted to be understood and known. Ultimately, they desired Jesus, not me.

For the last five years, I have continued to make videos, and I continue to receive heart-felt emails. The number one question I still get today is, "How are you always so happy/joyful?" I usually internally laugh as I read the message because I am not ALWAYS joyful. However, I do choose to see the joy in every moment, including my darkest one, loneliness. It took so much of my life captive!

That is why, for Christ's sake, I delight in weaknesses, in insults, in hardships, in persecutions, in difficulties. For when I am weak, then I am strong. (2 Corinthians 12:10)

If there is one verse that mirrors Finding Joy in Loneliness, it is this one. We can find joy in our hardships and difficult moments because when we are weak, God is strong. To this day, I am still learning what God is teaching to me. I don't know all the answers, however, I do believe that this book was fully God-breathed. He led me through every single chapter, and trust me, He definitely writes better than I do! (I can barely write an Instagram Caption!)

My hope for this book is to bring new life and joy in your moments of loneliness. I hope our hearts and love for the Father would deepen and cause us to look to Him fully, in all of life's difficult moments. I hope you will walk this journey with me and taste and see just how good the Lord is.

Taste and see that the Lord is good; blessed is the one who takes refuge in him. (Psalm 34:8 NIV)

Love,

Britt

1

ABANDONMENT AND ADDICTION

Creating the Facade

I'll never forget the first time my sister and I watched a rated-R movie. We were at our aunt's house and I probably wasn't more than twelve years old at the time. The truth is, I don't even remember what the movie was about. What I do remember is that this was the weekend that my sister and I were supposed to spend with our dad. Instead, we were dropped off at our aunt's house so that he could go to some party. As much as I love my aunt, this isn't how I envisioned spending my first day back with my dad. I thought we would go out to dinner, or get ice cream and catch up on how we were, but we didn't. Instead, my sister and I were sitting on a couch, trying not to focus on the inappropriate movie that was playing in front of us.

Even through disappointment, I kept a straight face and pushed my emotions down. I had to. This wasn't the first time I had to either. I needed to protect my younger sister from the pain of feeling abandoned, and I believed I had the ability to do so.

Growing up with my dad not being very present was challenging. I saw him on special holidays and some weekends, but that was about it. My mom and dad divorced when I was two and soon after, my mom moved 4 hours away. It wasn't my dad's fault that we lived far away, but it almost seemed like day after day we became less important.

As the oldest sister of three, I put a lot of responsibility on myself. Since I could remember, I always made it my job to protect and shield them from any and all hurt. Of course, as a young child, that was impossible and it only caused me to suppress more pain.

During my adolescence (2 - 12 years old), I had a stepdad. He taught me so much of what I know now, and he really was, in my eyes, a great dad. Although, there was so much I didn't know about him as a child because my mom wanting to protect us. I won't go to deep into it, but it became a whole 'nother trauma-filled story.

We ended up packing our bags and leaving him in the middle of the night because of the unhealthy situation in which we found ourselves. I don't know much about that night, the why or the before my mom woke us up, but I'll never forget my step dad being on his knees, in the middle of the road. He was in front of our car pleading for us to stay. I was heartbroken seeing my step-dad like that. Like I said, I love my step dad, but I had no idea the brokenness and addictions he was caught up in that affected my mom. Now as an adult, I understand it needed to happen. After that night, I didn't hear from him for years.

Growing up without either of my dads caused me to often feel unwanted. I desperately desired my dads to be a part of my life, to know my school grades, to care about my interests, or to pick up the phone and just call me, but that rarely happened. Sure, my mom was there—she was great! I love her with all my heart. But nothing could fill the void of wanting my dad to be a part of my life.

Since my mom had to fill the role of both mom and dad, this caused her to put on a strong face, similar to mine with my sisters. Because of that, when I was younger, we didn't talk much about emotions in our home. Knowing this about my mom, I tried to be the best daughter and sister I could be. However, that only pushed my emotions down further and began callousing my heart.

Later in life, through counseling, I learned that putting on a strong face was one of the many masks that I wore in order to protect myself from the trauma I was experiencing. I subconsciously wanted to be like everyone else. At first, knowing about putting on a facade made me feel as if I had been deceitful, but later I learned that putting on masks is something many people do without even realizing it. As days went by, it became easier for me to be someone I wasn't. The enemy had persuaded me to think that by stuffing down my emotions, I was protecting myself.

I think my mom was aware of our broken hearts. She would comfort my sister and me when we were disappointed with the visit with our dad. Although, with me trying to be strong and her protecting us, vulnerability wasn't much of a thing in our household. Most of the time, I was left alone with my thoughts:

Were anyone else's parents divorced? Was I different? Could anyone understand me?

I felt alone in my emotions and in my heartbreak. I wanted my dads to care about me. I thought that if either of my dads would do those things, maybe I wouldn't feel so alone?

- *What are some masks that you wear in your personal life to protect yourself?*

The Deeper Issues

Feeling alone was only a part of the deeper issues going on in my heart. The more my two dads neglected to be a part of my life, the more I felt rejected.

The deeper issues growing in my heart caused me to ask myself more questions.

Was I not good enough for my dads? Was I unlovable? Did my dads ever love me?

Even if I *was* good enough for my two dads, this was the lie the enemy continued to whisper. This small lie that I believed about my relationships with my fathers continued to bleed into other areas of my life—my identity as a daughter, my identity as a student, my appearance, my friendships. I felt like I was inadequate in every part of my life. This lie affected my friendships negatively and became an obstacle to feeling loved by others. I thought no one wanted to be friends with me or wanted to love me. I subconsciously told myself, *I'm unlovable.* I had friends, but there was always an inner voice telling me I wasn't good enough, I wasn't loved, I didn't matter, and I was forgettable. I developed codependent tendencies early in life because I wanted acceptance so badly—to be loved and to be enough.

While in middle school, I searched for love through relationships. I wasn't allowed to date until I was sixteen, but I did have a few boyfriends before then. (Sorry Mom!) If a boy liked me, I saw it as an opportunity to be loved. I believed if a boy liked me, I was "good enough". When my mom found out I had a boyfriend, I had to break up with him. My worst fear was losing the person I believed held all my value. I didn't want to lose someone who chose me. I was devastated whenever I didn't have a boy in my life to validate my worth. I believed if a boy didn't desire me, I had no value. Although at the time, I couldn't put these feelings into words. I just craved the attention I was getting and wanted to continue fulfilling it.

When ninth grade came around, I was finally able to date! I had at least six boyfriends at different times that year. I went from breakup to new relationship—always moving on to the next boy interested in me. The disappointing truth is that even when I jumped from boyfriend to boyfriend, my perceived value and worth continued to diminish. During that time in my life, I would likely do anything a guy told me to do. This led to some dark days filled with sneaking around with friends, going behind my mom's back to spend time with guys I liked, and putting myself into compromising situations—all to feel loved and accepted.

- *What or from whom does your value come from?*

- *How has that affected you?*

This boyfriend cycle continued until the fall of my junior year. Sadly, looking back, I'm not even sure I actually liked any of the guys I dated. I often ask myself what I saw in them. They were mostly jerks that I had nothing in common with. Truthfully, they only offered me what I *thought* was value. Things began to change when I met my husband, Connor. He was a sophomore and I was a junior in High School. Connor was a charmer. He didn't seem like the other guys I met before. He was respectful and kind. He even brought me to his church. He was perfect!

The Hidden Identity

Later I found out, Connor had a hidden identity. Although, realistically, I knew he had shortcomings, I refused to see them because again, someone loved me and gave me value. During this time, he struggled with alcohol and had a nicotine, and pornography addiction. At the beginning of our relationship, he would lie to me about small things and I chose to look the other way. I wanted to see the best in him and didn't understand addictions yet— I knew nothing about them—so I overlooked the lies.

As a new believer, I started seeing my worth and value as a young woman. So when I knew Connor lied, I broke up with him. However, coming from a sheltered home and not understanding addictions, as soon as he said he stopped, I took him back. This meant he needed to lie more so I wouldn't suspect anything.

EVEN AS A
CHRISTIAN, THE
HURT WENT ON
FOR YEARS
I DIDN'T
UNDERSTAND THE
Healing Power
OF JESUS YET.

Even as a Christian, the hurt went on for years. I didn't understand the healing power of Jesus yet. I was trapped, seeking acceptance and love from anyone—especially a man. I couldn't escape the vicious cycle of what loneliness and the lies of the enemy were doing inside of my heart. The abandonment, the hurt, the lies, I suppressed them all. I kept desiring the unconditional love of a man, expecting him to give me value and make me feel less alone. Little did I know the unconditional love and value from God that I would step into later in life.

- *Think back to a time when you distracted yourself with busyness to avoid dealing with what loneliness was doing inside of your heart. What patterns do you notice?*

give
it to
God

Prayer

Dear God, I am so hurt and I feel so alone.

My value and my worth are rooted in everything except You.

Is it wrong for me to want to be loved and wanted? My heart aches from the disappointment that is all around me. My heart has grown calloused from protecting myself from all of the disappointment in my life. I don't know how much more I can take and that makes me feel inadequate.

Help me to see You in the midst of this. Help me to see my true value. Unravel the pain in my heart and use it to make something beautiful.

Lord, I ask that You would send Your Holy Spirit to heal me of the things I have stuffed deep in my heart for so long. Heal my broken and burdened heart. I want to see your goodness in this, but I just can't right now.

In Jesus' name, amen. 💙2016

PERSONAL PRAYER

_____

_____

_____

_____

_____

_____

_____

_____

_____

_____

2

THE TOXIC MARRIAGE

A New Stage of Loneliness

Connor and I got married on May 8, 2015, after dating for almost five years. We spent the first year of marriage apart. I was in Texas finishing my last year of college while Connor—in the military—was in San Diego at his first duty station. Our first year of marriage was not only difficult because of the separation, but also because we were constantly arguing. At this time, I had no idea why our marriage was so hard. I kept telling myself that things would get better with time.

Since so many people in my family were divorced, I was familiar with the hurt it caused and I wanted something better for myself. I didn't want to repeat the generational curse of divorce. I wanted things to be different, so I created a fantasy of a perfect, fairytale marriage. I wanted a marriage where we went to church together, had deep and meaningful conversations, and loved each other unconditionally. However, I didn't even know what a perfect marriage looked like, nor did I know what unconditional love looked like.

To make sense of everything, I created a marriage mirage—one that looked like we were in total agreement from the outside when, in reality, I was only being passive. I overlooked red flags to avoid conflict. I also looked past selfishness and our surface-level, pointless conversations. I needed to believe that I married the perfect man. After experiencing a few months of constant arguing, I realized not only the brokenness I married into, but also, that which I had been carrying around with me my entire life. I too lived in brokenness from past sins that had been stuffed down. I think I hid the pain because I thought I was different. I didn't want to be judged or rejected again, so I believed ignoring it would make me like everyone else.

Discovering my husband's addictions put me in a new place of loneliness, but so did the walls I built around my past. It was at this point I started to seek out counseling. However, new questions continued to arise.

Am I the only one dealing with a broken marriage? Could anyone relate to the loneliness I felt?

Every young marriage is "happy and full of life," or so I thought. The shame and guilt I put on myself only led me further into isolation. Likewise, Connor's addictions pressured him to disconnect emotionally.

- *Identify a time when you felt like you were the only one that knew what it was like to deal with a certain situation. How did you feel during that time?*

- *Did you feel outcast or separated from others?*

Learning About Addiction

Through my life experience and time in counseling, I learned that addiction caused Connor to think he was coping and emotionally connecting with me, when in reality, he was isolating himself from the people he loves. This became very destructive to the relationships in his life, especially ours. Addicts become addicts to avoid their emotions altogether, but it only causes more physical and emotional damage that, particularly with porn, they are unable to see. At the time, it felt like Connor's heart had grown so hard and calloused that my anger and tears meant almost nothing to him. I could yell, scream and weep until I had no tears, but still nothing. I didn't understand why or how he could be so cold. Most days, I would sit quietly crying on the floor in our bathroom. With my face buried deep within my knees, I felt completely alone in my emotions.

After completing college, I moved to be with Connor. Things got worse. I was in a new state, away from friends and family, dealing with my marriage that was on the brink of divorce. While trying to keep our marriage afloat, there were days when I was literally alone because Connor was gone for training (known as an underway). Shortly after moving in with him, I went into a state of extreme sadness. I wouldn't say I was going through depression, but I sure was close. I had no friends or family living close by, my husband was still dealing with addictions, and on top of that, he was gone all the time. I was left processing my emotions in an unhealthy way.

- *Identify a time you felt alone and found it hard to process your emotions in a healthy way.*

- *Were you stuck, wanting to walk through it with someone who could relate to your circumstance?*

The Loneliness of a Military Wife

As hard as my marriage was at the time, being a military wife added a whole 'nother level to the conflict and loneliness I was already experiencing. I was alone most of the time since Connor was gone for days and sometimes weeks during his underways. So basically, within the first few days of living together as a married couple, I had to learn how to live alone while also being far away from any friends or family. This was a challenge for me, because I had never lived by myself. Before I married Connor, I lived with my family and had roommates throughout college.

Now, I feared for my life as I slept in a bed without Connor, hoping no one would break in. (This was probably my own fault for watching *Law & Order: Special Victims Unit* and *Criminal Minds* at ten o'clock at night).

I didn't realize being a military wife would be so hard. I feared for his safety each time he left, while simultaneously fearing for my own. As our marriage continued to get worse, worry and control became my go-to feelings. I was afraid that Connor would cheat on me because our marriage was already messy. I worried I wouldn't be able to make friends, find a job, find a church to plug into, and I didn't want to walk into a church by myself. Anxious thoughts consumed my mind each moment we were separated. The enemy was most certainly winning and he knew it. He had isolated me to the point of hopelessness and I continued to spiral towards anxiousness.

As a new wife in a new state, I was terrified of growing apart. I didn't know anyone, and he was my everything! I think this was also a big fear of mine because I already felt so physically and emotionally alone. I felt alone whether he was home or away. As empty as I felt, everything in me needed to cling on to the one man I believed truly loved me. If my codependency wasn't bad already, it sure was getting there.

One of my go-to verses during that time, and to this day, is Matthew 6:34 (NIV).

ALTHOUGH I COULDN'T SEE IT THEN, SEEDS WERE BEING PLANTED IN MY HEART AND THE *Spirit of God* WAS ON THE MOVE.

It says, "Therefore do not worry about tomorrow, for tomorrow will worry about itself. Each day has enough trouble of its own." Every day I would recite that verse, even in the midst of my constant worrying. Tears would run down my face at night as I began to memorize it. It was the first verse I ever truly memorized. Although I couldn't see it then, seeds were being planted in my heart and the Spirit of God was on the move.

(One of my favorite things about this verse, is that it doesn't say there won't be "trouble" or things to worry about. However, it does say that in the middle of those daily worries, let us be present. Present with God, and not focused on the future. I also love to read Matthew 6:25-34. It reminds me of how faithful our God is, always leading us through difficult times.)

In preparing this book, I found the following Scriptures to be helpful.

Read through each scripture and:

- o   highlight the verse that speaks to you most in each passage.

- o   Memorize the verse that comforts you most.

- Matthew 6:25-34

- Deuteronomy 31:1-30

- Romans 8:18-30

- Philippians 4:4-9

One of the crazy things about being a military couple or even in a long-distance relationship is that you believe you are expert communicators. Military couples, when apart, must communicate through writing emails and letters or sometimes being able to talk on the phone. Although it seems like a lot of good communication options, the reality is that there is so much more to communication—most significantly, that of vulnerability, which we were not yet practicing. Connor would leave and we would continue to exchange letters, emails, and phone calls; yet each day, we continued to grow further and further apart with our surface-level conversations: How are you? What did you do today? How was school?

This cycle continued for another year. We tried to keep our marriage from falling apart by going to counseling and marriage classes, but then he would leave. We would lose all the progress we made, and the arguing would begin again. It felt like three steps forward, two steps back. Looking back, the days weren't all bad. We most definitely loved each other (or what we thought was love) and that's the reason why we continued to fight for our marriage.

The months leading up to Connor's deployment terrified me. Oh, and guess what, we moved AGAIN. This time Connor was stationed in Everett, Washington, where I didn't know anyone and Connor was always gone at training. However, we were making great progress working on our marriage and learning how to communicate when he was home. Even with moving to a new state, I finally felt like our marriage was starting to heal. But of course, like always, Connor was going to have to leave again and this time for 6+ months. My heart's desire was to continue growing in communication and healing with my husband, but it almost seemed pointless, since he was just going to leave again. Fear of the unknown left me questioning if my marriage was going to survive this deployment. It had already survived so much hurt that I was slightly confident in it, but we had also never gone that long without communication. The feelings of abandonment were triggered in me once again. I felt sick.

Triggering Past Abandonment

All of these emotions continued to revive the pain I felt from my fathers, which didn't make life any easier. Neither one of my dads came to my wedding, and that made me feel abandoned by them all over again.

My biological dad decided to stop speaking to me before our official wedding ceremony, which was in May. So when my birthday came in August, it had been four long months since we last spoke. All-day, I waited for his call. Connor made the day special for me, but my heart still hurt from the disappointment of not yet getting a call from my dad.

Later that day, Connor and I went to our church groups. Mine happened to end a little early so I went and sat in the car, alone. I was waiting for Connor as well as a call from my dad. Knowing he probably wouldn't call, I was still hopeful he would. The call never came. Honestly, it wasn't even my birthday that I cared so much about (although I *do* love my birthday). It was mostly the pain of feeling so alone and rejected. All of the men in my life seemed to have abandoned me. So, I just sat there, sobbing in the depth of the pain I was living, questioning the relationships in my life and if things would ever change or get better.

Every day leading up to deployment became more terrifying than the last and I felt more alone. At the time, Connor had no idea how scared or abandoned I felt. Or at least I thought he didn't. I don't think I even knew how I felt because I was still learning how to process emotions with my counselor. Connor and I would have small conversations about what we were feeling, but I never felt like he fully understood me. Looking back, I don't think I even tried to understand him. I was so focused on my own emotions. I assumed he felt he needed to put on a strong face so I wouldn't be afraid of what could happen to our marriage, or more likely, the stress and loneliness he would also be dealing with.

Changing My View of God

Unable to process my emotions with Connor and the fear of him leaving soon, once again, left me feeling abandoned in life and in my emotions. I used to depend on Connor to be my comfort ever since meeting him in high school, which was almost six years ago by this point. Now that he was about to leave, I realized the only comfort I had in those moments was the Lord. I'm not going to lie, realizing the Lord would be my only comfort was kind of "ugh." He had been my sideline option for so long, I wasn't ready to ONLY have Him.

- *Have you ever gone to a friend for comfort before going to The Father? If so, can you think of a time where it would have served you well to go to The Father first?*

- *In whom or what did you find comfort in your times of struggle?*

Mentally, I always knew God to be Comforter, but now it was as if God was deepening, within my heart, the image I already knew about Him to be true. He didn't want me to swing back and forth from Him to Connor. He wanted all of me. He wanted me to see Him as greater than my circumstances, as Father and Comforter, but I didn't see that yet. My counselor at the time continued to lead me back to the book of Psalms. David is constantly in distress, and yet, he cries out to the Lord *knowing* He will comfort him.

"Your promise revives me; it comforts me in all my troubles." (Psalms 119:50 NLT)

"When doubt filled my mind, your comfort gave me renewed hope and cheer." (Psalm 94:19 NLT)

I love the confidence David has in the Lord. He continuously trusts that the Lord, *alone*, is his comfort. Not Connor, Netflix, or Instagram…like I often believed. I could and would no longer be able to find comfort in my husband because he would be gone. I didn't feel ready to enter into this difficult season, but God was about to change everything I knew about Him and the comfort He brings.

- *Reflect on a time when God was comforting you without you realizing it.*

- *What do you think God is trying to reveal to you about your struggle with loneliness and/or abandonment today?*

give
it to
God

Prayer

Dear God,

I am here again, this time, filled with shame and worthlessness.

Why am I continually abandoned by the men whom I love? Why do I have to feel so alone? I don't want to walk this road alone.

I don't know how to walk in this marriage, carrying all of the pain from my past. My load is becoming too heavy to carry and I can't do this alone. My mind and body are exhausted from all of the weeping and long-suffering. I'm so tired from trying to hold myself together and I don't think I can do it anymore. I want the men in my life to change, but I also know that I need to change, as well.

Comfort my broken heart, God. I am reminded of what David wrote in Psalms and I mirror that prayer and request. "Your promise revives me; it comforts me in all my troubles" (Psalm 119:50). "When doubt fills my mind, your comfort [gives] me renewed hope and cheer" (Psalm 94:19).

I need Your comfort, Father. I desire the hope and joy that only comes from You.

In Jesus' name, amen.

♥ Brittani

PERSONAL PRAYER

_____

_____

_____

_____

_____

_____

_____

_____

_____

_____

3

THE RELATIONSHIP

Establishing a Foundation

On June 1, 2017, Connor left for deployment. By this point, I had already decided to stay in Washington because I felt the Lord was leading me into a potential job and new friendships. The decision was very difficult for me. I heard that military wives often go home when their husbands deploy to be close to family, but for some reason, God was telling me to stay. I'll be honest, I really didn't want to. The thought of staying gave me a knot in the pit of my stomach. I was afraid, but at the same time, I could feel God wanting to teach me something new. I just didn't know what that was yet.

Here I was again, learning to be alone in a new state, only this time I needed to do it for six to eight months. Being a military wife is a lonely experience. Mostly because we struggle connecting with others. We're constantly moving, constantly trying—or not trying—to connect, because we are hoping to find people who will understand us and the lifestyle we live. The struggle to connect often results in more isolation. We end up either giving up or being tired of the constant "get connected" cycle. However, this time, in this new state, I was determined to find a community.

During our first week in Washington, we discovered that we lived right next to a church. Within two weeks, this church became our new church home. Literally. We walked in our first day there and the connection lady said, "You want to come to our life group Christmas party?" "Uhhh, yeah, sure, okay!" We were excited but nervous! We have never found a place so loving, life-giving, and relationship-oriented. It obviously was no coincidence that we found this church, but when deployment finally came, I began to pull away from the community God had for me.

Going to church alone is difficult. Walking in by yourself, even if you know a few people, is hard and somewhat terrifying. Not to mention, the sidewalk to get to the front door of our church is SUPER long and intimidating! There were many weeks where I watched online and isolated myself. In every way, I was fighting the idea of being alone.

The first few weeks of Connor being gone caused a tornado of emotions. The built-up anticipation and anxiety of him leaving was finally released, but there was also the heartbreaking reality that I was now going to be alone. My conversations with God looked like fits of anger with tears streaming down my face, and sometimes there were moments of stillness where my tears naturally fell out. I began the journey of experiencing true deployment loneliness and I wasn't ready to face the months ahead of me. The fear of the unknown seemed the most terrifying to me. I took God off the throne of my life and put myself there. With no control of the unknown, I began to panic. I had no idea how I was supposed to live without my husband for 6-8 months. He was my rock. He was my person, and now I had no one—or at least thought I had no one.

- *Have you ever been upset with God? Why were you upset with Him?*

God Opens My Eyes

It wasn't until Connor left that God opened my eyes to a Scripture I had read and seen many times before. In that state of loneliness, God brought me to the story in Genesis 2. It was one of those days where I forced myself to open my Bible out of obligation. I was sad, lonely, and empty, and Netflix bingeing definitely wasn't working. So, I opened my Bible and for some reason, a God reason, I opened up to the beginning and found myself in Genesis 2.

Opening this chapter was interesting to me because I've read this story a million times, like many of you probably have. We all know, "In the beginning," and how Adam and Eve were created. However, this time the words, "It is not good for man to be alone. I will make a helper who is just right for him," jumped out at me. The simplest phrase brought me the most meaningful message. I understood that God wanted Adam to have a partner just like every other creature, but what I hadn't yet grasped was the deep and intimate relationship that God desires with all of us.

It wasn't just the union of marriage but also the union of partnership and friendship—with God's purpose and intent for man/woman to not be alone. Now, I know what you are thinking because I thought this too. *How can we find joy in loneliness if God created us for relationship?* This is where I found myself to be stuck. This is where my anger and tears came from. I continued to read, "it is not good for man to be alone," and cried out to God, saying, "THEN WHY AM I ALONE?! Why have you allowed this situation, a broken marriage and now a deployment, to be a part of my life?" It was in those tears and anger that He revealed the deeper message of relationship to me; Relationship, not only with your spouse but with community. This was the foundation of the journey on which He was about to take me, but first, He needed to establish His powerful truth. Relationship is important!

- *In your deepest moment of loneliness, which relationship did you seek out?*

Something Is Missing

By now, I had retreated into isolation mode, thinking thoughts I believed I had overcome: *no one can understand, no one cares, no one is going to like me in this new state.* When we moved to Washington, I decided that this time would be different. We would be active in our church, have friendships, and get involved. However, as soon as Connor left, I lost the motivation for it all. It even took me some time to begin reading my Bible again, but God knew what I needed and when I needed it. The simple verse from Genesis 2, which I read many times before, began to breathe life into my struggling faith. It was still scary for me to step out of my comfort zone and into these new relationships, small groups, and military spouse meet-ups, but God equipped me with the courage to do it. Every day I filled my time with relationships. The more relationships I engaged in, and the more I got out of my home, the better things became, or so I thought. I needed to stay busy and I needed to engage in relationships. This forced me out of my house and gave me purpose, even when I didn't want to get out of bed.

But still, something seemed missing. Busyness consumed my life. As busy as I made myself and as much as I filled my time with people and relationships, I still came home to an empty house. I would be alone with my thoughts and often cry or numb myself to sleep by scrolling through social media.

What was I missing? I did what You wanted me to, God! I am in relationship with people. People who love You and encourage me. But here I am, at night alone, crying because of the loneliness I experience every day!

This continued off and on for a few months. I would meet with friends, go to church, be in the Word, but then I would pull away, isolate, and cope in unhealthy ways. Friendship wasn't enough for me and I thought it was supposed to be!

Relationship With Him

It was at that point, God revealed to me the deeper message behind Genesis 2. Relationship with Him. It was as if He wanted to show me the importance of relationship and community, but also that those couldn't replace the relationship we're supposed to have with Him FIRST. And of course, He brought me back to Genesis, a book I thought by now I mastered in understanding.

This time He highlighted Genesis 2:7-8 (NIV), *"Then the LORD God formed a man from the dust of the ground and breathed into his nostrils the breath of life, and the man became a living being. Now the LORD God had planted a garden in the east, in Eden; and there he put the man he had formed."*

As soon as Adam was created, God gave Him purpose and identity. I don't know what your story looks like, but up until this point, and even during this time, my purpose and identity were rooted in anything and everything, including, friendships and community. As important as these things are, I placed all of my worth in them.

Throughout the Bible, God would show me the moments where He met people while alone, giving them purpose and identity.

And when Elijah heard it, he wrapped his face in his cloak and went out and stood at the entrance of the cave. And behold, there came a voice to him and said, "What are you doing here, Elijah?"

He said, "I have been very jealous for the LORD, the God of hosts. For the people of Israel have forsaken your covenant, thrown

down your altars, and killed your prophets with the sword, and I, even I only, am left, and they seek my life, to take it away."

And the LORD said to him, "Go, return on your way to the wilderness of Damascus. And when you arrive, you shall anoint Hazael to be king over Syria. And Jehu the son of Nimshi you shall anoint to be king over Israel, and Elisha the son of Shaphat of Abel-meholah you shall anoint to be prophet in your place. And the one who escapes from the sword of Hazael shall Jehu put to death, and the one who escapes from the sword of Jehu shall Elisha put to death. (1 Kings 19:13-17 ESV)

...HE MET PEOPLE WHILE ALONE, GIVING THEM *purpose* AND *identity.*

In this passage, we see Elijah in distress, overwhelmed about a situation. God asks him, "What are you doing here?" followed by giving Elijah a new purpose and identity!

Then there was the story of Moses. God almost always spoke to Moses alone to lead him into His purpose.

Then Moses went up to God, and the LORD called to him from the mountain and said, "This is what you are to say to the descendants of Jacob and what you are to tell the people of Israel: 'You yourselves have seen what I did to Egypt, and how I carried you on eagles' wings and brought you to myself. Now if you obey me fully and keep my covenant, then out of all nations you will be my treasured possession. Although the whole earth is mine, you will be for me a kingdom of priests and a holy nation.' These are the words you are to speak to the Israelites." (Exodus 19:3-6 NIV)

The LORD would speak to Moses face to face, as one speaks to a friend. (Exodus 33:11 NIV)

- *What do you think the Lord is showing you about your purpose and identity?*

Purpose and Identity

In this new season of loneliness, God was teaching me an abundance of new things. One fundamental thing God taught me was that He would use my state of loneliness to lead me into His purpose. I definitely wasn't feeling joy in it yet. I still thought loneliness was the worst!

However, as God continued teaching me these things, He started to reveal the special moments that I got to sit with Him. Through these moments, I was able to find purpose and identity in Christ, in the midst of the unknown, the anxiety, and the fear. Slowly, but surely, my identity no longer came from others. As I sat with Him, reading His Word, my identity became more rooted in Him and my purpose became clearer.

As transformation began to take place, I thought, "Yes, my husband is still someone I love deeply, but he is no longer my rock." God became my rock. God is who my strength comes from. He is the one who calls me daughter, redeemed, courageous, and chosen. I was put in this situation, in the midst of loneliness, to find my Father—to find my identity—to find healing, without knowing at the time, end up writing this book so you too can find freedom from wounds that are rooted in loneliness.

- *When was a time you felt separated from God?*

The Fall and Separation From God

The second thing God opened my eyes to was that He too experienced the feeling of separation. The earliest moment of this occurred in the garden in Genesis 3. While walking in the garden, God asked Adam, "Where are you?" Adam had been hiding from God, in shame, after being deceived by the enemy into eating the fruit from the tree of good and evil. God didn't need to know where Adam was because He is God. He knew exactly where he was. The real reason God asked about Adam's whereabouts was because God immediately felt separated from His creation. There was a missing part—a brokenness He felt. God was already hurting when asking Adam where he was.

Truthfully, God cannot be in the presence of sin. When Adam and Eve initially let sin enter their hearts, it broke the Father's heart to banish them because of His desire to be in relationship with them. Throughout the Old Testament, we see that the people of God had to continuously offer sacrifices to God to be in His presence. However, God ultimately wanted complete wholeness and to restore unity with us.

The reason God sent His One and only Son to die on the cross was so that He could be the perfect sacrifice to restore the relationship He wants and desires with us. Through this, we see Jesus' separation, while alone on the cross, having purpose and identity. He needed to endure the pain of separation and sin on the cross for the purpose of restoring complete freedom and unity, which we now get to experience with the Father.

These biblical truths drew me closer to the Father. I finally understood that the God of Heaven and Earth intimately knows and sees me. He sees my hurt but also, He too experiences hurt in longing for relationship with His children. The harder thing to acknowledge was that just as I was hurting from the separation with my husband, God was hurting from me turning my back on Him. I realized I was just like Adam in Genesis 3:12 when he blamed God for his own actions. "It was the woman *You* gave me," Adam said. My blaming God often looked just like that. "This is the situation *You* gave me." "Why am I always alone?"

Unfortunately, getting to this place of realizing that God wanted a relationship with me first took months. For months, I created a life of busyness, filling it with activities, friends, and a dash of Jesus every now and then. Not until the last half of my husband's deployment did I realize how much God loved me and wanted to spend time with me. The most heartbreaking thing the Lord convicted me of was that the time I spent wishing I could connect with my husband was ten times less significant than God's longing for me. God longed for us to connect, have intimate conversations, and just be in each other's presence. If God was my first priority, as I claimed, then why was I neglecting Him and only desiring and waiting for my husband? This is when my journey of seeking the Father above all else began.

- What does your relationship with God look like at this moment? Is it a passionate pursuit or a dash of Jesus every now and then?

give
it to
God

Prayer

Father God,

Here I am, alone again. You've called me to stay in Washington, but I'm anxious about what the future holds. I'm scared of being alone, while Connor is gone.

Help me to draw closer to You during this time. I thank You for sending Your Son, Jesus, so that we can be in relationship with You. I thank You because, through Him, we are now made righteous and Holy. I thank You for creating new life in me. Even in my anxiety, I am reminded that the old is gone and the new has come. Help me to live in the truth of Your Word, that I am righteous and holy and made perfect in Your image.

Help me to trust Your plans for my life and believe the promises of Your Word. Thank You, Father, for continuing to show me Your goodness and mercy, even when I am angry. Thank You for loving me through my negative attitude. Thank You for the community that You have given us. I pray that I would not isolate myself, but dig deeper into relationships that draw me closer to You.

In Jesus' name, amen.

♥Brittani

May 27, 2017

PERSONAL PRAYER

_____

_____

_____

_____

_____

_____

_____

_____

_____

_____

4

THE RETREAT

Resting with Jesus

A few months before my husband returned home, late 2017, God began to show me the *beauty* of loneliness and how to cope with it. What actually happened was that I finally began doing what God was calling me to do. I could tell you that coping with loneliness was easy, but if I did, I would be lying. It was difficult. I was terrible at it one day and did awesome the next. It was definitely a learning process that I had to go through, but the Lord was patient and kind with me each step of the way.

He showed me how to be intentional with my time. Have you ever tried to be intentional with your time when you were in the midst of loneliness? It is so difficult! I would rather be a couch potato, watch TV, and scroll on social media for hours instead of, literally, anything physical. Would a walk be amazing? Yes! Would going to the gym be beneficial? Yes! Yet, in the midst of loneliness and trying to be intentional with my time, those positive activities seemed to become more dreadful to think about (While the couch became the comfiest place ever!).

I knew I needed to be intentional with my time, but everything inside of me wanted to fall into old patterns of unhealthy coping, which sometimes I did! My flesh was fighting my spirit. It was during this time when God led me to the following verses:

"Rather, clothe yourselves with the Lord Jesus Christ, and do not think about how to gratify the desires of the flesh." (Romans 13:14 NIV)

"Do not conform to the pattern of this world, but be transformed by the renewing of your mind. Then you will be able to test and approve what God's will is—his good, pleasing and perfect will." (Romans 12:2 NIV)

These verses helped me realize that by believing the lies of the enemy and being lazy in my spiritual life, I was gratifying the desires of my flesh and I wasn't allowing the Spirit to renew my mind. I love my Heavenly Father and yet everything I did was to escape the pain in my own flesh. Escaping my pain only made me a slave to numbing it temporarily—a temporary fix that ended in me feeling alone again. Each day I worked towards changing the way I lived, and I began being intentional with my time. It reminded me of Jesus' relationship with the Father. Mark 1:35 says, *"Very early in the morning, while it was still dark, Jesus got up, left the house and went off to a solitary place, where he prayed."*

We see Jesus going to be alone, entering into the presence of the Father to pray. His time alone was ultimately not spent alone, but in unity and relationship with God. Each morning Jesus chose God, knowing He would be incomplete without Him.

Being reminded of this, I began making small changes in my life. I wanted to be intentional with my time and to choose unity with the Father. I wanted to feel incomplete without the Father. So I began taking walks, going to the dog park more often, and breathing in the fresh Pacific North Western air. I took moments to watch the birds and be thankful for every creature in the sky and every plant on the ground. I took small steps to love each moment of my day and to be aware of the things around me. I began to see from a Kingdom perspective by looking at the blessings of each moment of my life. I was unaware at the time, but looking back now, these were the special moments I began seeing God in my loneliness.

- *What does unity and relationship with God look like to you?*

Women's Retreat

A few months after my husband came home, I was still determined to dive deeper into what God was showing me. I found out my church was going to be hosting a women's retreat and a few of my friends were going, so I decided to sign up. I was never a fan of women's retreats. I remember going to one with my mom when I was younger. It was just a one-day retreat, but as a teenager and new believer, I found it to be kind of boring. Some things said were good and I'm sure my mom loved it, but it wasn't something I can say was memorable.

The women's retreat I went to however, was beautiful! It looked like a spa and a cabin campsite rolled into one. Absolutely gorgeous. This women's retreat was supposed to be a time of intimacy and rest with Jesus. Do you know what that means? At the time, I didn't. But I went hoping to learn all the things I could do to achieve that!

One of the first things we were told when we got there was, "This is a time for us to rest." I got that, but who really rests at retreats?

"If you want to sleep through a session, do it."

Wait, what?!

"If you want to walk alone and take some time for yourself, do it."

I was shocked, but also excited.

I still hadn't grasped the meaning of resting with Jesus, and even though I thought I did, I was excited to learn what it truly meant. This retreat was different, and I knew God was about to teach me something new. On the second day of our retreat, we listened to an awesome speaker named Paula Gamble. She taught us a lot of great and powerful truths about what it means to sit and be still in the presence of God. For a Biblical example, we can look at Matthew 11:28-30 (NLT): *"Then Jesus said, 'Come to me, all of you who are weary and carry heavy burdens, and I will give you rest. Take my yoke upon you. Let me teach you, because I am humble and gentle at heart, and you will find rest for your souls. For my yoke is easy to bear, and the burden I give you is light.'"* My favorite section of this verse is "Let me teach you." God never intended for us to come to Him knowing all the answers. He wants every part of us, and for our hearts and souls to find rest in Him.

The story of Mary and Martha includes this key verse as well: *"Her sister, Mary, sat at the Lord's feet, listening to what he taught"* (Luke 10:39 NLT). If you are unfamiliar with the story, it is about two women, Mary and Martha. Mary sits at the feet of Jesus to listen to Him, while Martha is busy preparing food. When I hear this story, I instantly condemn Martha. Why would she be preparing food when Jesus is present? Why would she not be at His feet, listening to Him? Although I condemn Martha, the spirit often reveals to me that I do the same thing. I create a busy life, full of things I believe *need to be done* out of obligation, or just plain ol' distractions. Even when I had the opportunity to sit at the feet of Jesus, I unintentionally chose otherwise. I took my focus off of Him for so long that it became my normal. This was going to be a challenge for me, but I was excited to refocus my spirit and soak up His presence.

- *Who do you identify with more, Mary or Martha? Why?*

After Paula finished talking, she told us we were going to do an exercise. We were to sit in silence for ten minutes (The recommended time was twenty minutes or more, but ten minutes was where we started), only thinking about one thing. It could be any one thing, but the focus was to be something spiritual. I chose Jesus. She told us that if anything else crossed our minds, we could capture it, throw it out, and refocus— staying focused on the one thing we chose.

Most of the women in the room had never sat in silence only thinking about one thing. Before this moment, *I've* never sat in silence and only thought about one thing in my life, *ever*. And yet, there we were, sitting still, quietly with our eyes closed.

Throughout the first minute of silence, I immediately thought about a million things. Basically, the first minute was me getting a grip on all the thoughts I had in my brain. After I got a grip on my thoughts, I tried to focus. I pictured myself dancing with Jesus. I imagined us having fun, free-spirited dancing and slow dancing. Sometimes we would sit and face each other, but for the most part, we were just dancing. Every few moments, I would think about something random, like how I needed to buy milk. I would get distracted and my picture would fade, but then I would throw it out and refocus. After ten minutes of silence we were done, but I felt a beautiful sense of peace, freedom, and rest. My mind was renewed. It was the most rejuvenating thing I've ever done!

Paula went on to tell us interesting facts about silence and noise association. In a study done by the American Psychological Association in 2011, they found that noise pollution has been found to lead to high blood pressure and heart attacks, as well as chronic hearing impairment and overall decline in health. Loud noises can also raise levels of the stress hormones, adrenaline and cortisol.

A 2006 study published in the Journal Heart found two minutes of silence to be more relaxing than listening to "relaxing" music, based on changes in blood pressure and blood circulation in the brain.

- *Take five to ten minutes to focus on sitting with God. There's no wrong way to do it. Pay attention to each time your mind wanders so that you can refocus and come back to God.*

- *Write down any words that come to mind from your time with Him.*

The Secret Place

After sitting with Jesus in my time of silence, I remembered how much God longs for us to be in relationship with Him. To get to know a friend, you sit with them. You take them to coffee and get to know who they are by sitting quietly and listening to them speak. So why wouldn't we do the same with God? How can we expect to get to know God if we are always running around, ignoring Him instead of listening to Him speak? In His presence, I get to hear and experience the depth of His love for me.

Through this experience, I learned that I need to be more intentional in my quiet time. Not just by sitting (and most likely getting distracted), but by intentionally focusing and looking only at Him. This was my "secret place." A phase I had never understood until now.

> *"He who dwells in the secret place of the Most High Shall abide under the shadow of the Almighty. I will say of the LORD, 'He is my refuge and my fortress; My God, in Him I will trust.'"* (Psalm 91:1–2 NKJV)

This was my place to abide and dwell in the secret place of the Most High. It was and is here that I find freedom from all distraction and disappointment. All I needed was to lay at His feet and rest, giving Him ALL of me.

There Are No Rules

I was never really good or consistent with journaling when I was younger. I would start a journal and write, "Dear diary, today was really hard" or, "Dear Jesus, This is how my day went." I wrote for a few days and then would pull away. I put so much pressure on myself to be consistent every day, but then, when life got too hard, I bottled things in and stopped processing with God. Journaling became a burden instead of a chance to share my heart with the Father. I felt like journaling was part of the *"good Christian"* packaged deal and yet I felt ashamed that I wasn't who I thought I needed to be. It wasn't until the end of deployment and then again at this retreat that I started to learn how to journal.

I learned the rules of journaling at the retreat. There are no rules. Put anything and everything down on paper. If you want to start with "Dear Jesus," go ahead. If you don't want to start with, "Dear Jesus," don't! Write every thought, feeling, and emotion down on paper. Meditate on Scripture. Question God. Write out a prayer you are too afraid to speak. Cry on the pages. Let the words reflect what your heart is feeling. If you miss a day, that's okay! As long as you spend time with Jesus, he doesn't care how you do it. Being intentional with my time, journaling, and releasing those thoughts and emotions to the Lord has been eye-opening for me. Meditating on the Word of God showed me that I was never alone.

Everyone would say journaling is important, but I felt like there had to be more to it!

Why *is* journaling so important to God?

What I'm about to say blew my mind when God revealed it to me!

The *Bible* is a journal!

According to Dictionary.com the definition of a journal is, "a daily record, as of occurrences, experiences, or observations." Isn't that almost exactly what the Bible is? Throughout most of, if not the entire Bible, we see a record of occurrences, experiences, and observances, but particularly we see this in Psalms and in the New Testament, where Paul is writing to the church. *Illustrated Study Bible* says, *"The psalmer contains much information on music making in ancient Israel. The majority of psalms are songs of praise, thanksgiving, prayer and repentance. They are also historic odes that relate great national events."*

The book of Psalms is made up of a variety of messages and reflections. We see David journaling songs of praise to God in the midst of difficulty and heart-rending circumstances. Personally, as I read through Psalms, it's as if I am reading someone's personal journal. I'm reading through the pain and difficult circumstances they went through, the questioning of God, but ultimately God showing up through their faithfulness and patience. We even see David going through trials alone and on the run, and God meets Him in those places.

Throughout Paul's writings, we again see a type of journaling, but as letters to the churches. Paul is writing about his experience with Jesus while confirming and defending the gospel! One particular book that I love is Philippians. Paul is writing to the church of Philippi while in jail...alone. Even while in jail and being alone, Paul uses the word joy/rejoice in his letter 16 times! I mean being alone is one thing, but to be in jail finding joy?! We need to be like Paul, whose confidence and identity was fully in Jesus!

"Yes, and I will continue to rejoice, for I know that through your prayers and God's provision of the Spirit of Jesus Christ what has happened to me will turn out for my deliverance." (Philippians 1:18b-19 NIV)

We even see in Paul's writing his encounter with God while alone in jail. We see God give him a renewed identity and a purpose!

"The following night the Lord stood near Paul and said, 'Take courage! As you have testified about me in Jerusalem, so you must also testify in Rome.'" (Acts 23:11 NIV)

After seeing all of these verses, I realized then, and even more so now, that journaling is an amazing opportunity to pause and reflect on our daily lives. It's a chance to see the Spirit move within us and receive a heart of thanksgiving. In my experience, journaling has even been a chance to write out frustrations, only to come back to them days later to see how

God used that situation. It has the power to provide clarity in times of uncertainty and remind us to pause and listen for when God speaks. After sitting and processing with God, I discovered journaling was far more important than I realized and I was excited to continue!

Each thing God was teaching me continued to lead me back to an amazing and intentional relationship with Him. Relationship with God didn't have to be burdensome or boring, but had the potential to be delightful and free. Isn't it cool that He promises and delivers that to us?

> *"It is for freedom that Christ has set us free. Stand firm, then, and do not let yourselves be burdened again by a yoke of slavery."* (Galatians 5:1 NIV)

We were called to live and walk in freedom, not check a box from a list of duties that would create stress and burdens in our relationship with Him.

The Last Night at the Retreat

We ended our time at this retreat in a time of worship, reflection, and prayer. As I surrendered my heart during this time all I could think about was the pain it had felt over the last few years.

Relationship

WITH GOD DIDN'T
HAVE TO BE
BURDENSOME OR
BORING, BUT HAD
THE POTENTIAL
TO BE
DELIGHTFUL AND
FREE.

my fathers and my husband. I knew He wanted to heal it, but it still lingered.

I wanted to let all the hurt go and find freedom, but I didn't know how. As I sat with my tears, a friend approached me, sat down, and listened to what my heart was feeling. After I spoke, she began praying with me.

I continued crying from pain but also joy. Even in my beautiful moments of being alone with God, He revealed how important community and relationship is when His presence is in the middle of it. I will always remember the time she prayed with me, mostly because God's presence was real in that moment and His heart and love were reflected through my amazing friend.

After leaving the retreat, I felt empowered—not from my own awesomeness, but from knowing the Holy Spirit did something truly special that weekend. I now had tools to take home with me to learn how to cope with my loneliness and depend on God more completely.

This was just another seed God planted in my heart, leading me to put Him first and find joy in my loneliness.

If you have never taken an opportunity to journal in this way, we have given you extra pages to do so. Write anything and everything going on in your heart right now, whether it has to do with this book or not. These pages are yours and God's.

JOURNAL

JOURNAL

JOURNAL

give
it to
God

give
it to
God

Prayer

Hi, Father. It's been a while since I've taken time to talk to you.

Thank You for continuously drawing me back into Your presence. As You know, I am at a retreat. I know that the timing is no coincidence. Thank You for this opportunity to be alone with You. As I leave this retreat, help me to continue to pull away from my life to be with You. Help me to say no to the busyness and the demands of this world. Help me be excited to run away with You as You lead me into the secret place.

As I sit in Your presence, I am reminded of all the blessings You have given me. Thank You for this home. Thank You for Samuel. Thank You for Your constant love and presence. You always wait for me patiently. Continue to soften my heart so that I can choose and pursue You always. Give me a kingdom perspective so that I can see You move. Thank You for Your faithfulness.

In Jesus' name, amen.

💜Brittani

April 7, 2018

PERSONAL PRAYER

_____

_____

_____

_____

_____

_____

_____

_____

_____

_____

5

UNRAVELING OF THE SPIRITUAL DREAM

God Speaks in Loneliness

Never in my life did I think I could find joy in being alone, or at least what I thought was being alone. As cheesy as it sounds, God *is* always with us. Yet, we fall into loneliness when we don't recognize His presence around us.

We have an awesome opportunity to experience His joy in our loneliness. When we begin to see our loneliness as a beautiful gift from God and an invitation to be in His presence, our focus changes. It's no longer wrapped up in the selfish nature of how we feel, but in the purpose and excitement of hearing from God.

One of the last times Connor was gone while in the military, he was gone for a few months. During those few months, I experienced loneliness again. In fact, I was writing this book! I say this because it's a journey...it's not something you learn completely overnight. However, this time, I recognized the loneliness and I decided to do something about it. So, each night I sat in the presence of God. I read my Bible, closed my eyes, and meditated on His Word. The first night was the hardest. Even though it had only been a few weeks since I was intentional with God, I could already feel the distance I created between us. My flesh reverted so quickly to only finding joy in moments I spent with my husband. Now that my husband was gone again, I found it hard to find joy in being alone with God. I know that sounds bad, but it was true for me at the time! However, as I stayed committed to the relational journey, each day I felt Him more and more. Having joy in His presence was revived.

After a few weeks, I experienced God speaking to me through a dream! Now, I understand that lots of different thoughts could be going through your mind right now. If you are a new believer, this might sound a little scary, *or* it may excite you to know how God can speak to us. You could also be very skeptical, which I'd understand. Trust me, I've been there. But being someone who dreams just about every night, I can testify that this is real. Another time God spoke to me through a dream was in high school, so I was familiar with the experience. When I woke up, I remembered every second of the dream.

- A few dreams that occurred throughout the bible.
  - ○ Genesis 28:12-22
  - ○ Genesis 37:1-10
  - ○ Genesis 41
  - ○ Matthew 1:18-24

- *Have you ever had a time where God spoke to you? What did you feel like He was saying?*
  - ○ *If not, sometime today, sit with Him and ask Him to speak to you. This will help you practice for when He wants to speak in the future.*

THE DREAM

The dream began with me on a scuba diving trip. It was the instructor, a boy, and me. I stepped out of the cool ocean onto the warm, dry land. I remember our flippers hitting the warm sand as it stuck to us. The hot sun was shining down, into our eyes so I knew it was almost the afternoon. When I looked around at the sand, the tall, tropical trees, and into the horizon, I knew we were on an island. However, as I looked around to make sure we all made it to shore, I realized only the instructor and I were there.

The little boy that was with us was missing. I looked at and around the instructor, but I didn't see the boy. I didn't see him anywhere. Frantically, I began searching for him. The instructor turned to search for him also, but unlike me, he was calm. I wondered why the instructor wasn't frantically looking for the boy. The boy could have been dying underwater! When I looked at the instructor, he was so calm and collected, carefully looking through the waters and toward the horizon. As I began searching also, I ran through the water and put my head under to see if I could see anything.

Nothing. He was gone. All I could see was the murky shore water in front of me. So I gave up looking. I said to the instructor, who continued to look, "The boy is gone. What's the point in looking? There is nothing we can do."

But the instructor continued to look in the water and toward the horizon. As I stood safely on the shore, the instructor continued to search for the boy. He walked in and out of the water, waiting to see some sign of him. Then out of nowhere, a hand shot up from the water. The arm frantically waved from left to right. As the instructor saw the hand, he reached out his hand to grab the boy from the water. Wading through the chest-deep water, he saved the boy. All of a sudden, I felt like I could feel what the boy was going through. It was as if I was now looking up out of the water as the instructor was reaching down over the water to grab my hand.

As the dream continued, the boy was now a man, sitting beside me on the beach. The man seemed to be my age. We were sitting on a log that was right next to the shore, looking out into the ocean and preparing to have lunch.

As the man pulled out his lunch to eat, I noticed he was eating a scorpion taco, an *actual* scorpion in the taco! It had claws and everything, and not even any cheese! (I know, silly. I could not understand yet, what God was trying to show me there!) It seemed to be completely normal, to both of us, for him to eat that. I was not eating with him because I was trying to pull a rope out of my body. Every inch of the rope was thick, rough, and full of seaweed. One end of the rope had an arrow tied around it and the other end was deep within my body tied around my heart.

My goal was to throw the arrow. I had no idea why it was my goal—I just knew I had to do it. One thing I did know was that I had to untangle the rope first because the knot was too entangled to easily pull out of me.

So as we sat on the beach, the man ate his very strange scorpion taco and I continued to unravel and untangle this rope within my body and around my heart. We never talked, just focused on our strange circumstances, sat on the log on the beach and stared out into the ocean.

When I woke up from this dream, I was amazed that I could remember everything. My dreams are usually all over the place with different scenes that I can only partially remember, but this dream was completely clear! Before I began processing the dream with God, I sat silently in His presence. I wanted Him to be fully a part of my understanding of the dream without my own imagination trying to control it. Truthfully, I had no idea where to even begin. I had never asked God to reveal the meaning of a dream to me before, but here I was, on my bed, hoping that this time, God would allow the Holy Spirit to reveal His message.

PROCESSING WITH GOD

As I was processing my dream with God, He began unraveling the details of it to me. I thought this was so amazing because before this I had struggled to sit in the presence of God for a mere ten minutes. I began to experience joy in my quality time with Him. This is what He means in Romans 12:2 by "renewing my mind."

First, I needed to learn what it meant to sit in the presence of God, because it would ultimately lead me into understanding the second part of Romans 12:2. *"Then you will be able to test and approve what God's will is—his good, pleasing and perfect will."* I've always known that God longs to speak to me. But as I was sitting on my bed that morning I realized that in order for me to hear, I needed to renew my mind first.

THE INTERPRETATION

In the beginning of the dream, as I was coming out of the water, with my instructor (Jesus) and into the sunlight, God revealed this to be a representation of me coming out of sin and turning my back on anger, insecurity, and loneliness. However, God was also revealing Connor to me. Connor was the little boy, childlike in his faith, and still struggling to step out of sin and into the light. He was being held in bondage by the enemy. The part of the dream where Connor was lost in the water was a reflection of my heart's attitude toward my husband. In our personal lives, I searched for him, or helped him overcome sin, until it became tiring for me. Out of anger and frustration, I gave up hope in trying to help him.

God was revealing a hardening of my heart toward Connor. Although, at this point in our marriage, Connor's heart was pursuing Jesus daily, it just wasn't up to my "standards."

The instructor (Jesus) continued searching for the boy (Connor) even after I got tired and gave up. God was showing me that even if I were to get frustrated and turn my back on Connor, He would never turn His back on him. Jesus would constantly pursue him, just like He constantly pursued me. While looking for and then finding Connor, He left me safely on the island. This picture mimicked the parable of the lost sheep.

"Suppose one of you has a hundred sheep and loses one of them. Doesn't he leave the ninety-nine in the open country and go after the lost sheep until he finds it? And when he finds it, he joyfully puts it on his shoulders and goes home. Then he calls his friends and neighbors together and says, 'Rejoice with me; I have found my lost sheep.'" (Luke 15:4-6 NIV)

God already had me safely in His presence, but because one of his children was lost, He did whatever He needed to do to find him and bring him back into His presence.

The next part of my dream was the hand that shot up out of the water. Connor was underwater in sin, scared, and in need of his Savior. God's response is always to rescue and redeem. This is a parallel to when Jesus pulls Peter out of the water. Out of fear and the need to control his own life, Connor lost sight and trust in Jesus and took his focus elsewhere. But Jesus is always there to look for him, find him, and save him. Today as I write this book, Connor has found freedom in many areas of his life. The man he once was in chapter 1 is long gone and being rescued from the depths of drowning in his sin. He has found freedom in Jesus. What was also interesting in the dream was that I then became the boy. At first, I thought this was to show me Connor's point-of-view, but then God revealed that just like Connor needs Him, so do I. I need Him daily, even if I feel "safe on the shore." And really, if I feel safe, it's because I am wrapped in my Father's arms and under His protection.

As I continued to sit with God, I began processing the second half of the dream. I was skeptical. I thought there was no way God could actually give me a meaning behind the scorpion taco, but He did. He was revealing to me that Connor was willingly being fed the lies of the enemy. What was interesting was that I thought it was normal. It could have been that I too, had been fed lies from the enemy before and knew exactly what they looked like. Later something amazing happened! Connor revealed to me insecurities he had been feeling and not sharing with me.

Lastly, the rope tied to my heart with an arrow at the end symbolized the boldness God wanted me to step into. He was telling me, *"All the hurt from your past, anger toward your fathers—I want to set you free. I want to untangle the gross rope filled with sin and bring into the light all the pain and shame trapped in the shadows of your heart. I want you to step into who I have called you to be, a bold and brave daughter."*

- *Who do you identify with today? Brittani, Connor, or the Instructor?*

REVELATION OF JOY

As I sat there in the quiet place of my heart, I realized I have never had a spiritual dream while Connor was home. God used moments of being alone to speak to me. It's not that God can't speak to me while Connor is home, but truthfully, I don't think my ears are as open when he is. When we open our ears to what God has to say, everything changes. Transformation happens, ideas are formed, and lives are changed! To clarify, I'm not saying that God will speak to everyone through a dream, because God speaks in many ways. What I am saying is, if you do find that God is speaking to you, make sure to listen very closely because it won't be a loud voice.

Then the LORD said, "Go out and stand on the mountain before the LORD. Behold, the LORD is about to pass by." And a great and mighty wind tore into the mountains and shattered the rocks before the LORD, but the LORD was not in the wind. After the wind there was an earthquake, but the LORD was not in the earthquake. After the earthquake there was a fire, but the LORD was not in the fire. And after the fire came a still, small voice. When Elijah heard it, he wrapped his face in his cloak and went out and stood at the mouth of the cave. (1 Kings 19:11-12 NIV)

Seeing what God could do in this moment of loneliness and stillness revived my spirit. In each of the moments where I found "joy" on my own, I had forgotten what true joy looked like. In my chaotic and fast-paced life, I had created happiness for myself that was fleeting. It was easy to grab on to those moments and tell myself the lie that I was a "joyful" person when on the inside, I was broken. God saw that and He wanted me anyway. He wanted me to *be* that joyful person, instead of the fake happy version I created for myself. He wanted me to experience Him and His everlasting joy.

Looking back, I can see how God was transforming my heart. It never really looked like transformation in the moment. Transformation looks painful, hard, and scary. Trusting that God can take my brokenness and create pure and unshakable joy seemed unrealistic, but He did it! I came from a place where I would never sit for longer than a minute in silence with God, and now I'm listening and hearing Him interpret my dream. God did that in me!

He transformed my view of everything I believed to be impossible in my own heart and revived my spirit. I was experiencing true, everlasting joy!

Through my experience, I know He can do it for you too! As someone who was not raised to have a relationship with Jesus, I saw God as a sideline option. He was someone I would

SEEING WHAT GOD COULD DO IN THIS MOMENT OF *loneliness* AND *stillness* REVIVED MY SPIRIT.

go to if I needed my sins forgiven or for whatever other reason I had.

I didn't see Him as someone who could give me complete and total joy. When I became a Christian, my views of God were still limited. I couldn't fathom the fullness of His glory just yet. My faith was focused on Jesus, who died on the cross for my sins, but what I was forgetting was WHO sent Jesus. God, The Father! I didn't know The Father. I didn't know His love and passion for my heart.

Over the past few years, my Heavenly Father has redeemed and restored my heart, bringing beauty and identity into the places I thought would forever be broken and dark. In this moment, as I am writing this book, there are still hard days where I fall short. But I know now where my hope, joy, peace, and patience come from. They are not from the things of this earth; they are in the everlasting. They come from my Heavenly Father alone, and I pray and hope you will find those in Him too.

give
it to
God

give
it to
God

Prayer

Dear Heavenly Father,

I thank You for this day and the new mercies that You provide each morning.

Father, today, I come to You with a dream; a dream that I believe is 100% from You. Please reveal the meaning of this dream to me. Reveal your heart to me as we process this together. I believe that behind my dream, there is a meaning that You want me to see. As I just sit and rest in Your presence, send Your Holy Spirit to fill my mind with Your wisdom. Make my mind wise and discerning enough to understand what You have for me in this dream.

Thank You, Father, for transforming my time with You. I now see the beauty of Your presence. Thank You for the ability to rest in Your presence and to see further than my own eyes can see. Thank You for Your Kingdom perspective. I thank You for the things that You already revealed in the dream, and I thank You for my time with You.

In Jesus' name amen.

Your Daughter, Brittani 🩶

June 5, 2019

PERSONAL PRAYER

_____

_____

_____

_____

_____

_____

_____

_____

_____

_____

6

THE REVELATION

Where Our Loneliness
Meets Joy

If you remember from an earlier chapter, on my twenty-second birthday, I was sitting in the car, waiting for and anticipating my dad's call that never came. Even though it had been months since my dad and I last spoke, I still hoped that he would call me on my special day. As I sat in the car crying and disappointed, in retrospect, I'm thankful and will always remember what happened next. As I sat in the car alone, I clearly remember feeling God say, *"Happy birthday, Brittani."* I burst into tears. What once were tears of pain I felt from not hearing from my dad, were now transformed into tears from the beauty and presence of my Heavenly Father. He saw me and met me where I was, in a place of loneliness.

I was alone in my car, but I didn't feel like I was alone. I was weeping and in awe that God remembered my birthday. What seemed so insignificant turned into something much bigger. My mom used to celebrate our birthdays for the entire month. I love my birthday, but this time, it wasn't about that.

I wanted to be seen and known!

I wanted to believe that I was important and special to my dad...

That moment I realized something... I *am* important and special to my Dad!

My *Heavenly* Dad.

I felt like He was saying, this is the day I made to be special for you, my daughter. Before this moment, I didn't think of God as Dad. I knew God as Creator and Almighty. Present but distant. Now, I see Him as God, the Father. My perfect Dad. A gentle, compassionate, present and near Dad that loves me and holds me through it all. I will always treasure that moment in my heart because it was then I realized what joy in loneliness looked like. Although I hadn't realized it yet, this was a moment when He was there for me, as I sat alone.

- *Do you experience God as your Heavenly Dad? If not, think back to a time when you were unaware of God's movement in your life. Journal your thoughts below.* 🖤

Thinking back on my life, I'm grateful now to see God's footprints in so many hard situations. By my junior year of high school, I already had at least ten boyfriends or people I "talked to." (Remember that phrase? Is that still a thing?) Anyone who had the slightest interest in me, I clung to. Then, God led me to Connor. It was Connor who took me to his church, where I first met Jesus. I remember the dark worship room where we sang worship songs and tears rolled down my cheeks as I believed and accepted the overwhelming love and forgiveness Jesus offers us. Even before I entered that building, God knew me and was waiting for me. God accepted and pursued me even before I was a believer, using Connor to lead me to church.

Long after becoming a believer, I still struggled with my identity. The difficult thing about identity is that if it isn't completely rooted in Jesus, it can easily be taken from us. I am reminded of the very first words we hear from the enemy to Eve.

Now the serpent was more crafty than any of the wild animals the LORD God had made. He said to the woman, "Did God really say, 'You must not eat from any tree in the garden'?" (Genesis 3:1 NIV)

He makes Eve question herself.

- *Think of a time when someone doubted your recollection of what someone else said. How did that make you feel?*

Suddenly you think, "Well, maybe *I* heard wrong?"

But even in my identity loss and even in my newness of faith, when I look back, I can still see the Father present in my life. When I was in college, laden with the ultimate question of *Who am I?* I met new people, new friends, boys, discovered new clubs, enrolled in new classes and still I asked myself, *Who am I?* In the middle of this, God introduced me to my first mentor, Dawn. As flakey as I was as a new believer in college, she still consistently met with me to see how I was doing. She taught me about discipleship. She taught me about Jesus and who God says I am. God used her to speak boldly and challenge me in my faith.

Another way God revealed my identity to me was through two special women, one named Diane, and another woman also named Dawn. After I found out about Connor's struggles, I sought counseling. This in and of itself was orchestrated by the Lord. As a college student, I didn't have any money for counseling. Ten minutes down the road there was a church that offered free counseling, one in particular, who specialized in marriage, anxiety, and betrayal. She also referred me to a class on marriage where I met Dawn. Both women had been betrayed by their husbands. Both women loved Jesus with all their hearts. This was no coincidence. This was my Father. Again, I was seen by Him. He saw my needs and provided for me. It still took me years to be rooted in my identity. It was hard being the only one in a marriage growing in their relationship with God, but I believe God intentionally grew me first so that I could be rooted in my identity in Him. If Connor had grown first, I would have looked to him before going to God. Throughout my story, in the pain and the frustration of feeling like I was the only one trying, God was there. He was writing my story of dependence on Him—paving the way for me to see my worth and identity in Him alone. As much as I hated deployment at the time, God used it to bring so much healing into my life. God needed to separate me and Connor so that He could individually transform us.

- *Do you see your identity in the fullness of the Father? If not, where does your identity lie?*

Of course, once in a while, the enemy will sneak back up and try to shake me, but God continues to be louder in my life. Through each of these small moments, God was shaping my identity in Him. I now know that I am enough, not because I am, but because *He is.*

I am enough because I am made in the image of a *Perfect God.* I am enough because my Creator says I am. I am so valuable to Him that He sent Jesus down so He could be in relationship with me. Wrapping my head around this can be hard sometimes because it's so simple yet so uncommon. In a world of busyness and information, simple is hard to grasp. I am enough because He says I am. Period.

This concept became so much clearer after I moved to Washington. Every day I look out at the mountains and am in awe of their perfection and beauty. I remember that God looks at me in the same way. Those mountains weren't made in His image. I am.

So God created mankind in his own image, in the image of God he created them; male and female he created them. (Genesis 1:27 NIV)

I praise you, for I am fearfully and wonderfully made. Wonderful are your works; my soul knows it very well. (Psalm 139:14 ESV)

For those who are led by the Spirit of God are the children of God. The Spirit you received does not make you slaves, so that you live in fear again; rather, the Spirit you received brought about your adoption to sonship. And by him we cry, "Abba, Father." The Spirit himself testifies with our spirit that we are God's children. Now if we are children, then we are heirs— heirs of God and co-heirs with Christ, if indeed we share in his sufferings in order that we may also share in his glory. (Romans 8:14-17 NIV)

I'm happy to share that my husband and I now work on our growing marriage daily! We most definitely still fall short each day as well, but as far as the things he has struggled with— God continues healing and purifying his heart. My dads are in my life, too. The relationships are slowly being rebuilt, and healing is happening. I am more than grateful they are in my life again.

As amazing and awesome as these things are, only within the last year has this been a journey of complete healing and restored relationships. Something that I continued to wrestle with as I looked back on the pain that filled my life, was why God made me go through these things. Why doesn't He just heal my husband? Why doesn't He restore my relationships? Or the one I hear often from others, "If God is so good, why would he do _____?" I have to constantly remind myself that God doesn't *do* any of this. We live in a fallen world where the enemy steals joy. He steals and lies to our loved one, fathers, and even us. He destroys relationships, leaving them broken. *But* God restores.

We live in a fallen world where evil things happen. But God can use those things to bring healing and restoration back into our lives, ultimately leading others to Him as well. Everything God does for us is good. So as I battled with the whys—*Why God, is my husband just now being healed, or Why God, is my relationship being restored just now?*—I believe the answer is because I had to go through years of pain.

Through everything, God reminded me that He is enough for me. It was so clear to me, it was as if I could hear Him. *"Now, your heart wants only me. Pain will come, and your heart turns to me and is filled with joy. You no longer feel pain the same way, because my joy lives in you. My love is enough for you."* This became my truth. When my husband would leave for months at a time, God was enough for me. When my husband was home, but not present, God was enough for me. When I felt unworthy to every important man in my life, God's love was enough for me. He was all I needed from the beginning. As painful as it was in the middle of it, I was slowly freed from those feelings of being alone and not enough.

Even a few years back, when things were tough, God was and is *still* enough.

When I lived in San Diego during our first year of marriage, I would often get so mad at Connor that I would leave our home. Usually, I wouldn't get too far, but sometimes I would go straight to the beach to just walk.

Now, when I reflect on the pain that I've been through in my life, I am reminded of the times when I would walk alone in the sand. As I looked back, I would see what I thought were my own lonesome footprints. In reality, those weren't my footprints at all. They were God's footprints as He carried me through the sand.

God carried me through each season of life, whether I realized it or not. I never was alone, it just always looked that way to me. Now I can look back and recognize the safety and security of being wrapped in my Father's arms. I now see how much of the burden He carried for me.

I always used to hear the phrase, "God doesn't give you more than you can handle." I started to believe it until my situation just became too heavy, and I *couldn't* handle it. There is a lot I could say on this topic, but to sum it up from what a friend once told me, "No, it's not that God won't give you more than you can handle, but that God will help you handle all that you've been given."

Friends, our world is hard. Brokenness, heartbreak and loneliness are real, but they do not win.

God sees us and meets us in these dark places once we recognize our deep need for Him. He is the victory! ALWAYS.

Now, every morning when I wake up and my feet hit the ground, I am reminded of my Father carrying me through my day. I can choose to walk in my flesh and in my brokenness, or I can be carried through the day by Him. Even in the midst of our physical loneliness, we can trust that our Heavenly Father is waiting for us with open arms. He is ready to sit with us, dance with us, or cry with us.

So yes, the phrase I used so long ago, "I don't feel lonely because I have the Lord," was partially RIGHT! (As cheesy as 2015 Brittani sounds). When we've truly laid the burdens of our heart at His feet, He replaces those things with His abundant love and beautiful presence. Of course, every day won't look the same, and that's okay! We were never created to be alone and separated from the Father. So as long as I keep my eyes on Him, my perfect Dad, He will be all that I need, because my true joy comes only from Him.

give
it to
God

give
it to
God

Prayer

Dear Father,

Thank You for every season, chapter, and moment in my life. Some of the seasons hurt and were full of tears and anger, but You walked those days with me and never left my side. My tears were not in vain. You gave me patience, endurance, love, peace, hope, and strength to forgive. Most importantly, You opened my eyes to see that I am enough because You are enough. You were always enough. Thank You for all of Your blessings, Father.

Thank You for my earthly fathers and the many ways they have shaped who I am as a person. I'm thankful that they both led me to be the best version of myself, ultimately leading me to You, Father. You led me to see You as my perfect Father through my relationships with my earthly fathers.

Thank You for my husband and the marriage You have given us.

Thank You for transforming my heart to be the wife You have called me to be.

And most importantly, thank You for my eternal relationship with You made possible by the sacrifice that had to be made.

Thank You, Father, for pursuing my heart in times of peace and also in times of anger.

Thank You for carrying the burden of my heart and never leaving me.

Thank You for seeing more value in me than I saw in myself.

Thank You for creating me in Your image and likeness.

Thank You for holding me, now and for the rest of my life. I pray that I will continue to draw closer to You and see the joy of being in Your presence always.

In Jesus' name, amen.

Your Daughter, Brittani. 🖤 *2018*

PERSONAL PRAYER

_____

_____

_____

_____

_____

_____

_____

_____

_____

_____

*I would love to connect with you
and hear your thoughts on my book!*

      : *youtube.com/britcon2*

      : *youtube.com/brittanikrebbs*

      : *instagram.com/brittanialexandra*

      : *facebook.com/britandcon*

NOTES:

CHAPTER 2:

1. Matthew 6:25-34 NIV
2. Deuteronomy 31:1-30
3. Romans 8:18-30
4. Philippians 4:4-9
5. Psalm 119:50 NLT
6. Psalm 94:19

CHAPTER 3:

1. Genesis 2:7-8 NIV
2. 1 Kings 19:13-17 ESV
3. Exodus 19:3-6 NIV
4. Exodus 33:11 NIV
5. Genesis 3:12

CHAPTER 4:

1. Romans 13:14
2. Romans 12:2

3. Matthew 11:28-30 NLT
4. Luke 10:39 NLT
5. American Psychological Association 2011- https://www.apa.org/monitor/2011/07-08/silence
6. 2006 Journal Heart Publishing - https://www.ncbi.nlm.nih.gov/pmc/articles/PMC1860846/
7. Psalm 91:1-2 NKJV
8. Dictionary.com
9. Philippians 1:8b-19 NIV
10. Acts 23:11 NIV
11. Galatians 5:1 NIV

CHAPTER 5:

1. Genesis 28:12-22
2. Genesis 37:1-10
3. Genesis 41
4. Matthew 1:18-24
5. Romans 12:2
6. Luke 15:4-6 NIV
7. 1 Kings 19:11-12 NIV

CHAPTER 6:

1. Genesis 3:1
2. Genesis 1:27 NIV
3. Psalm 139:14 ESV
4. Romans 8:14-17 N

ACKNOWLEDGMENTS

Trish Perez, my friend, and editor: You made this book what it is today! Thank you for keeping my voice and style throughout this book. You allowed the Spirit to lead every conversation and chapter. I appreciate everything you have done!

Connor, my supporting and loving husband: Thank you for encouraging me throughout the whole process of writing this book and being open to whatever God wanted to share through it. Thank you for the late-night final edits and for helping me bring clarity to every chapter. I love you!

To my mom, Margaret: I love you so much! Thank you for all your support of this book. You have always encouraged me to pursue my dreams, and I have always looked up to the passion you have for accomplishing your own dreams.

To my Northshore friends and community: Thank you so much for your prayers and support through this journey! My relationship with The Father was deepened through how I saw Him

in all of you. I could not be more grateful that we were led here to Washington, by the military, and now have an amazing and life-giving community. Love you all!

Special thanks to my amazing friend Amanda Long for taking the cover photo of me! I am so grateful to have met you and connected with you. Your friendship, leadership and passionate heart for Jesus mean more than I can express! Love and miss you, Stewart and Quill!

Diane and Dawn R.: Thank you, from the bottom of my heart, for all you did. There is not a day that goes by that I don't live by the things you both have taught me. I am inspired and encouraged by your bold faith in Jesus and constant pursuit of Him. I will never forget how you both have impacted my life. Thank you so so much for all you have done!

To my Discipleship Mentor, Dawn W.: I can't tell you enough how much I appreciate you. You continued to push me to deepen my faith and step out into very uncomfortable, but spiritually growing places. There are so many great memories I have from discovering who Jesus was and is, with you. Thank you so much for being a disciple-maker and leading me closer to Jesus.

Special thanks to my Youtube family: You all are the reason and inspiration for this book and I could never thank yall enough, but I will try! Thank you for always believing and supporting me through all my big dreams!

Financial supporters:

Mararget Rodriquez, Mary Flores-Hayes, Teresa Del Pui, Jenny Krebbs, Fernando Tamayo, Ricardo Perez, Emily Rubatino, Karli Nelson, Lauren Stein, Chelsea Belverino, Serena Garcia, Katie Steele, Leah Yoder, Sydni byerley, Ratana Lieng, Ayonna Williams, Makenzie Bennett, Michelle Wilgus, Meredith Blair, Nichole Black, Scarlette Hermoza, Wanda Capece, Jadyn Bryan, Ashley Hortis, Tiffany Martinez, Kiara Hernandez, Mikayla Matheson, Maribeth Allen, Rebecca Peterkins, Haley Corder, Hannah Jenifer, Kelsey Ferguson, Julia McFarland, Brittney Roy, Heidi Sandee, Kelsey Keenan, Emily Minton, Joanna Lauby, Kelly Brady, Rae Atienza, Kristen Strange, Eve Vang, Emily Stephens, Cameron Shepherd, Jessy Gonzalez, Tovah Travis, Erica Calderin, Hailey Bunch, Sydni Byerley, Kylie Schmolitz, Ashley Penton, Leilani Monzon , Karina Olmeda , Victoria St. Amand, Molly Dempsey, Sarena Criger, Briana Bathauer, Alison Purtee, Mile Figueroa, Jessica Savitz, Julia Cheam, Makyla Tanner, Olivia Piercy, Iris Garcia, Maribeth allen, Berenice Nevel, Danielle Minich, Katie Stewart , Rebecca De La Paz, Hanna Norland, Rute Morais, Meghan Howie, Amy Merida, Jessica O'Brien.

ABOUT THE AUTHOR

Hello wonderful people!

Thank you so much for reading this book and even taking the time to read this very last section! I never in a million years thought I would write a book. To be honest, I am a slow reader. I get through maybe one or two books a year. However, one of my favorite things about taking it slow is that I get to soak up every piece of biblical truth. That is what I hope for you too. I hope you held on to the biblical truths and tucked them away in your memory for moments of loneliness.

A little bit about me, since loneliness is only a part of my story!

I'm married to my loving husband Connor, and we have a beautiful baby girl, Eva Grace. We also have a 5-year-old dog named Samuel. He is a small black lab, who has the energy of a puppy! I also work at Northshore Christian Church as an Online Media Coordinator! God has always given me a heart to share Jesus to the online community and I've loved serving and working there. During our free time, Connor and I love to take walks, go to parks and watch the Office for the hundredth time. (It just doesn't get old!) We currently live in Washington State but are originally from a small town in central Texas. My husband likes to joke with me and tell me I am turning into a true Washingtonian. Mostly because I eat healthier now and drink Almond milk. Haha! Sorry Texans, I just can't do Dr. Pepper anymore! Although, I will always love me some Whataburger.

That is a little bit about me! I would love to hear your story and connect with you as well! If this book impacted you in any way or you just want to chat about life, you can find my contact info below!

God Bless!

: youtube.com/britcon2
: youtube.com/brittanikrebbs
: instagram.com/brittanialexandra
: facebook.com/britandcon

JOURNAL

JOURNAL

JOURNAL